And Then She Persisted

by

Kenisha Coon, MS

Finishing Line Press
Georgetown, Kentucky

And Then She Persisted

Copyright © 2024 by Kenisha Coon, MS
ISBN 979-8-88838-596-8 First Edition
All rights reserved under International and Pan-American Copyright Conventions. No part of this book may be reproduced in any manner whatsoever without written permission from the publisher, except in the case of brief quotations embodied in critical articles and reviews.

Publisher: Leah Huete de Maines
Editor: Christen Kincaid
Cover Art and Design: Kenisha Coon
Author Photo: The Jonesy Co LLC

Order online: www.finishinglinepress.com
also available on amazon.com

Author inquiries and mail orders:
Finishing Line Press
PO Box 1626
Georgetown, Kentucky 40324
USA

Prologue

This is a warm message to those who may be reading this story, and thinking that they may have gone through so many things alone in their lives. You are not alone. I would not have been able to get my story out without the years of working on myself in therapy, working through my self-discovery, and my self-journey. This is for those who have overcome hard times. This is for those who are determined to make sure they are breaking the generational trauma of their families. This is not the "oppression Olympics". I am not sharing my story and journey to prove that I endured more than another individual. I am sharing because I wanted to share my truth.

This is my truth. No one can take your truth away from you. We are all on different parts of our healing journey when it comes to overcoming trauma and dismantling racism. I am very humbled that I get to share mine.

There are graphic instances in this story, some names have been omitted and/or changed to protect their confidentiality.

I am dedicating this story to Matthew, my partner and my biggest supporter, and my two amazing little men, Victor and Jaxson, who changed my life and threw me into the superspeed loop of discovering myself.

Lastly, I am dedicating this story to my determination and persistence. I would not be where I am today if I did not recognize that I could overcome and do something about it. I vow to continue to advocate, fight, and speak up for all of the other Black and Brown children who suffer from racism, abuse, and neglect.

And Then She Persisted.

1

I was born three months early on the 2nd of September 1988, in the city of Port Huron ~ Michigan. My mother should have originally given birth to me in November but could not, due to certain factors that happened a few hours before my delivery. The story told to me was abuse, abuse on my father's part, that had sent her into early labor.

I was born a 3lb (3oz) baby and spent several weeks, which felt like months, to my mother at the hospital, and was only eventually permitted to go home under keen supervision, and with the aid of certain heart monitor machines.

A heart monitor lay wrapped around my arm and connected steadily to my heart, and its seemingly mechanical contraptions had the duty of alerting my mother of any changes in my pulsing pattern as well as the doctors in charge of me. The machines were set up in such a fashion that curated any slight changes noticed about my health for the negative, and this would see me pay another expedient visit to the hospital, to stabilize my condition.

I also had breathing machines stuck to me as well. Excluding these aids stuck to me like a leech to a favorable host, and adding my scheduled bi-weekly checks to this exception list as well, I would still be a regular at the hospital nonetheless. I had a lot of surgeries in those first few months of my life.

The most vivid one in my memory, being told, was the double hernia repair, and exploratory surgery I had as an infant. I still bear the dark scar line it drew laterally, across the face of my abdomen. I remember staring blankly at it for long periods in the shower as a little girl, wondering why this happened to me, and thinking to myself, "How was I going to be pretty with this wretched thing on me?". It stood on my belly for a long time as the emblem or stigma of my frailty as an infant. It still stands.

The doctors told my mother that the hernias developed due to the complicated circumstances surrounding my birth, and I had to get the surgery done for this as well as quickly as possible at the time. Technically, I had two surgeries done on me, during the first few months of life within the space or time frame of about a month. It didn't take long, however, till I completely recovered and began a slow but steady shift toward normalcy.

After all these phases passed and I could now live with my mother at home without any machines stuck to my organs, I was given the name ~ Kenisha Ann Marie Williams.

And as though the name had defined my leap into maturity and had metamorphosed me to a certain degree of normalcy, I never really fell ill after these first few periods.

By looks, I was biracial. You wouldn't need a genie to tell you that I had a cross of parents in colors, one white and one black. And rightfully so, my Mother was White and my Father was Black.

Generally, it takes humans a while to fully adjust to new environments, even more so for newborns. What starts as just selfish craving for food irrespective of where or how it comes, suddenly grows with a realization of their immediate surroundings. This is relative to the family they have, their financial capability, and all other things after that. It didn't take long for me to become aware of my family and my environment as there was nothing to be aware of. We were poor!

For this reason, we moved from one house to another so many times while growing up. I cannot vividly remember certain houses or schools from my pre-middle school years. We moved so many times, that by the start of high school, I had gone to about 7 schools at the least. This came to a stop however once I got into high school.

In high school, we eventually settled down in a house, in the South End of Port Huron. The place was a tourist attraction site always buzzing with activity during festive periods of the year, and it was a really beautiful place. It still is actually.

The waterway that dumped into the lake, the serenity of the mornings as its residents went on early morning runs frequently, the bridges it had that led to Canada and was one of its easiest and most beautiful access routes across the states, or it's long, cold and dry winter that births extra snow every year from the lake effect. It was such a beautiful city, to live in and to grow up in. It is also the only place I vividly remember as my childhood home growing up.

My Mother always had us working hard in school, and we would always have no choice but to do so, as we knew where we had come from and the nature of things at home. Working hard meant homework and cleaning on repeat, starting at a very early age. Although, somedays just that and there were days we would go without food at all despite having food stamps from the government. Usually a punishment.

Despite the state of things at home, however, my sister and I would always try to understand that my mother was working multiple jobs each day to give us the best that she could.

During the beginning of my going to school, the teachers would usually tell my mother that they were sure I probably wouldn't fit in with the rest of the kids my age. This was a logical conclusion, seeing as I was quite smaller than my peers in size and stature, and looked the odd one out from a mile out. However, this changed with time, and I soon overcame the first waves of setbacks I was bound to face from being premature at birth.

It was only at the beginning that I had these complications with my health and wrestled fiercely for my life. After this, however, my first strides of genetic persistence paid off, and I was able to adjust to society just fine. I was born a survivor.

And then she persisted.

2

There are a few things you should know about my childhood in Michigan. Firstly, I never knew my father. At least, I was perceived to not know.

My Mother tells me he left before I was born and I always felt bad not having ever met him. I was always curious to know how he looked, what he was like, and if things would have been different if he were still alive and living with us as a family. Whenever I would ask my mother, she would tell me the barest minimum and it always felt like he left me, leaving us to be with another family. She never liked to talk about it. One thing she would always tell me though was that I was a spitting image of him facially, save for my skin. People, especially "friends" at school always said I was like an Oreo cookie (white on the inside and darker outside).

Excluding the fact that I never knew my father or anything about him except for the fact that he was Black, I could tell that he must have been abusive to my mother before he left her. My Mother always talked about him with such a distasteful look on her face but that wasn't the only reason I always thought of this. Primarily, my Mother was abusive.

Physically or verbally, my mother always abused my sister and me however and whenever she deemed it necessary to, which was often. She also usually never had a smile on her face.

My Mother beat me with anything she felt was sturdy enough to inflict pain, and she hit all parts of the body equally and fairly. She threw toys at us, lashed our backs with belt strokes, and hit our butt or thighs, or any part of our bodies within her reach at that time. The area she was hitting never really mattered to her as long as her message was passed. And she never stopped after a short whooping. She never also passed up a chance to show us that the point would get put across with physical anger. There were several occasions when I got hit for doing something naughty (usually mediocre and typical of a child) and she would hit me so violently, I would begin to think and feel like she was not my biological mother. She often made me feel like I didn't belong.

She would pin us down under her and smack the daylight out of us continuously till we were no longer crying from the pain but screaming for our dear life. Even to the point of being kicked down the stairs. There, in our house, abuse was normal. And it wasn't just my mother that was abusive. Looking back now, I wonder how someone could always be so angry and abusive with her children.

Whenever my sister and I had to visit any relative of ours from our mother's side, which was the only relative had anyway as my mother never told us about any of my father's relatives, we would always get beat up for the slightest possible thing. It didn't matter if we were kids or were just being naughty. The beatings would happen continually, in a similar fashion, and with the same result every time. We got knocked around so much that we developed a thick skin for it. By our grandmother, by our babysitter. It didn't matter.

There were certain times my Mother had to be at work for long periods running multiple jobs to shoulder the many responsibilities she had as a single mother and would not be home for an extended period. Rather than leave us to our devices during these times, she would elect to take us to our grandmothers, or would just give us to her best friend, especially when the prolonged stay of hers was short notice. And we would get physically and (usually) verbally abused in these places as well. They would put us in the corner for extended periods, sometimes until we peed our pants. We could never complain, lest we would get smacked for even causing trouble for being punished. To her, we were the cause of the problem wherever we went.

After some time, not until we were closer to adolescence, we grew to adjust to the beatings and the maltreatment others who used to beat us didn't bother us as much as they used to anymore. However, my mother grew more inventive as we sort of adapted to all the effects of her aggression towards us. She developed brand new ways to inflict pain on us in ways she felt were as effective as they could be. The abuse grew worse at this stage.

I remember getting kicked down the stairs or hit with various objects. My mother could make us go through anything at this point, as long as she felt that this method inadvertently hurt us more than the last one.

One of the most vivid examples of physical abuse I remember from these times happened to me when I was about seven. I had returned from school extremely hungry and decided to take some loose change from my mother's purse to go get something to eat.

When my mother returned and discovered what I had done, she told me what I had done was theft and first beat me up a little. Then, she heated up a penny on the kitchen stove till it was red hot and she made me hold the penny in my hand for as long as she wanted. I yelped in excruciating pain.

She told me that if I let the penny out of my hand to fall on the ground, I would get hit and she would heat the penny all over again for me to hold. Whatever pain you imagine this felt like isn't even a fraction of the real thing till you multiply it by threefold at least. Living in that house in those days was hell.

And then she persisted.

3

In America, and as a biracial child, you get to experience bits and pieces of racial aggressions, racism, and this convoluted sense of degradation by society and from people you know (or may not know) daily. This is the first formal appearance of these types of treatment by kids between the ages of seven to eleven, especially in schools, and the racist slurs or statements (be them intentional or unintentional) usually start to develop and become normalized at this stage of middle school and high school.

In my case, I didn't have it all bad, at least at that adolescence age, I did not think that it was that bad. My school was not extremely diverse, but in most cases, it was racially accepting despite it being quite populated by White folx and barely having a handful of people of color in attendance. I think now that I might just feel this way because I lacked the understanding of what racial aggressions and racial slurs sounded like. Whenever I would hear these words and feel hurt, I never really understood why I felt that way on the inside. These people did to me with their active or passive statements most of the time because it questioned my identity and origin.

People would unapologetically call me "Black on the outside and White on the inside", and would pull my hair or stroke it without permission in a bid to touch it, or feel its texture and girth. Then there was the folk, who would tell me that I was the "Whitest Black girl they have ever met."

The foundations of the American educational system were already deeply rooted and infested with systematic White supremacist values long before any of us were here. We would learn bits and pieces of history that always portrayed the Americans and their wandering origins in light, and would never do justice to the barbaric nature of their colonial efforts, and the oppression the Native Americans faced at the time.

Additionally, there was no expansion on any Black historical figures whatsoever thus leading figures or study cases like Martin Luther King, Nelson Mandela, Rosa Parks, or later, Barack Obama, as a single topic study and these would be hugely glossed over in such a controlled fashion that have children the impression that these names were just honorable mentions and nothing more.

When we did get taught something, it was either well-worked lies about Christopher Columbus and the real story of the genocide agenda or how he did certain things he didn't do. These stories always glossed over the horrible things he did in the name of discovery and colonial efforts, and this still went on in school for a long period till the walls of systemic White supremacy and racism began to get hit and dismantled in recent times due to movements like the Black Lives Matter protests and these such movements been to pave the way for change, and look beyond a hate/racist infected society to one of tolerance, equity, and justice.

But before all of this, the change was seemingly impossible, unreachable, or worse still, unattainable. This might have been birthed from the fact that I had not one Black teacher at this time and as I remember it from grade school until I graduated high school. It wasn't till I got to junior college that I had my first Black teacher, and this should speak volumes, she was the speech professor. It was not until I was well out of college that I got formal education on the level of Systemic White Supremacist values that were embedded in the roots of the United States and that had eaten so deep into it, they had made their way to the educational sector as well.

This racial oversight in my schooling days got to the way we were treated, the way we were grouped and thus affected the people who made friends with us because children can always see and feel the disconnect between cultures portrayed by the society, and they are never attended to imitate it as quickly as they could.

To be fair, the White kids only sat around with the White kids, and the same was respective to the Black kids as well in class while a teacher taught or during lunch breaks in the school hallways, and nobody batted an eye at this or called it out as wrong or improper because it was the societal norm at that time. Even I didn't realize there was something wrong with this arrangement till later on in my studies with racist benefits portrayed consciously or unconsciously by societal forces and strata. This was how severe this was, the systematic racism indentations.

During athletic activities, I would see teachers encourage the White kids who looked like them to work harder and move faster, but would also (probably) degrade the Black kid standing next to this White kid in the most appealing ways possible; and it's usually difficult to spot what things to protest if one felt like they had been wronged.

The White kid usually for "Aww shucks, you can do better and you will next time", while the Black kids would get told in front of the entire class "well she's Black, and she has to be that fast", and these little racial oversights end up becoming the big brick of racially constructed aggressions and polarity towards people of color by these White kids over time.

I would get told things like "You're pretty or smart for a Black girl", and "you're different from us, are you adopted?" (being adopted is not a negative, I just was not)and I would have no idea how to respond to these comments because I had no one to confide in whether I got back home from school each day.

I remember there being days when I actually would consider the possibility of wanting to be adopted due to the way my mother treated me as a child. I would see the lifestyles and desires of other children in my school or my circle and these would reaffirm my thoughts of wanting to get out every time.

And then she persisted.

4

When a snail feels it is in danger, it usually hurls itself back into its shell. It considers this a safe space. Similarly, when humans feel threatened about their immediate surroundings, they tend to discover outlets to channel their frustration or anger, usually productive or negative.

This was my situation and thus, this was my solution.

When the aggression and anger caused my mother to continually inflict pain on us, I knew I needed a way to escape. This was where I began to ask questions that only music could answer. I began to rely on music.

I would always be secluded, alone in a secret space somewhere in my room, listening to a song from the Backstreet Boys, Nsync, Brandy, Britney Spears, Janet Jackson, or Michael Jackson. I had these headphones I loved so much that were extremely loud. I would always put them on indoors, and play them as loud as I possibly could, using the music to drown out the sorrow that I had felt for several months and years on end. All of that negativity was taking a gradual toll on me psychologically and physically, and I barely even knew what those were then.

This was primarily because most of the abuse did not stop till I was in high school and its effects continued up to when I was an adult and I was able to fend for myself. They still affect me in a sense until this day.

It must have been around this period that I began to grow farther and farther away from home as I could no longer feel the warmth of the place or the love that anybody had for me. At that time, it never really felt like home, and I never felt like I was with family.

I never really wanted to come back home and I want to spend more time in school. This is also when I began to join every music class that I possibly could.

Choir and Guitar were more or less an outlet for me to escape. I didn't have to go back home as early as I normally would to escape my mother's madness or anger and frustration, and most times I would even extend this stay to other clubs as well such as the drama club.

I would join every possible music class that I could, including being a teacher's aide for one, as well as drama club's late meetings and rehearsals, just to get extended amounts of time that I could stay there, without having to go home early. I just thrived for this extra moment being excited, spending time doing something that would ground all of the pain and the possible anger that would be taken out of me if I had gone home earlier. Most of the things I was here for I didn't even remember them but I remember the pain in my head because most of the time the negative outweighs the positive.

This was also when I started to buy things myself. This was when I got my first job.

Now, we grew up poor.

Getting basic amenities was the most important thing to my mother and getting anything else was like a wish made upon a well. She made us understand fully well and quite early, that she could not provide anything else outside her basic responsibilities, and there was nothing we could say to her that could persuade her to change that. It just could not happen. Whatever it was you were looking for, wishing for, your request would most definitely get rejected.

This is why I knew I had to get a job when I turned 14 and I did get a job at McDonald's, not too far from the house. I worked here for about 5 years, and I enjoyed the work that I did here, particularly making me ascend the promotion ladder, till I could no longer work there anymore. I was made manager, then shift manager, and got to be in charge of a lot of things and people, and got to interact with people in the truest ~ most meaningful sense as well. My first real taste of leadership that I have taken with me to this day. I was always putting all of my energy into everything that I did.

If I was to pick a particular reason for my emergent affinity to this place, it would be that I was looked at here as a person, and could communicate as such without having to get defensive of anything or shut down for something I may or may not have done. It was the comfort of this place and ethics and values that made it more homely and hospitable than my own mother's house, that made me give my all to the actual success of that place, and ensured that I was one of the best working staff there till I decided it was time to leave.

These facts however only stood relatively true to this particular establishment because I may have been able to do the job to the best of my capabilities as well.

Alongside the job at McDonald's, I was always trying to get a second job that would inadvertently increase my finances and therefore my earnings, and so I went around at some point in time, trying to land myself a second job.

The first job I tried to get was at a daycare not too far from our residence in Port Huron at the time, and it was a demanding job. At the start, I liked it and wanted to do well there as I have always had a passion for children's welfare and growth generally as a young child. Unfortunately, my stay here was a short-lived 6 month period, as I couldn't properly deal with the stress of two full-on jobs alongside getting my desired grades in school, and the fact that I had gotten strep throat 3 times in those 6 months, I had to quit earlier than I had ever expected.

After this, however, I soon landed another job at a consignment store, where I was finally able to settle down, to toggle both jobs together, to achieve my desired midpoint in the balance between my success at school, and enlarging the depth of my pocket by expanding my financial pool. With this, I was able to get myself most of my wants and needs, without having to rely on anybody other than myself for a long period. I also got to work at a consignment store and there, we dealt in clothes, conveying, logistics, and so on, and I would treasure every opportunity I got to talk to a customer and immerse myself in the job very seriously. During these periods, I was never home but I was always happy. Maybe these two occurrences were mutually inclusive events during these times.

When I was 12, I met my best friend Tawny. Tawny and I came to like each other almost immediately after we met. We would spend so much time together. We would spend the weekends together or I would stay the night at her house. We shared a locker for years and we would write notes back and forth with our notebooks that we still cherish to this day. I know for a fact she still has those notebooks. We would have the best of time, we did this for years and we learned to grow with each other.

She was also one of the reasons why I was able to stay at school and was able to endure the racial slurs and racial aggressions that I seldom faced as a biracial child all while facing my studies squarely, and doing the best I could to make my dreams come true. Although a majority of these incidents left trauma indents in my brain, she was one of the reasons I was able to contain it to a considerable extent till I started going to therapy later in my eyes and I begin to understand those things I thought were normal and that I could surprise you at really not supposed to be suppressed and why not normal. She knew, and still currently knows every single detail about me and my life

She was my joy repeatedly, and I owe a lot of my persisting zest to her support and thoughts towards me. She still is 25 plus years later.

It was during this time that I began to look beyond the physical abuse that seemed to discolor every day I lived with my mother in that house. I had to discover an outlet, a channel of sorts I could use to suppress or blacken out the effects of the abuse on me psychologically. It was around this time that I became dependent on music, choir, and drama club. I used them as an avenue to avoid going back home early after school or going to school late in the mornings. I took multiple choir classes and a guitar class. I learned how to play the guitar a bit, and I started to go up on stage from there to perform with my class members whenever I got the chance. At this time, I joined the drama club after school hours. After finishing up early from extra choir activities, I would hop right over to the drama club. I stayed away from home for as long as I possibly could in those days, and only came back when I was almost sure my mother was asleep or not around, and I would not get hit for doing anything again. I just focused on being my person at this point.

The mentors that I gained during this time, for this particular point in time, were exactly who I needed in my life at those moments. My Choir teacher, Mr. Beasley, let me know that I could amount to anything that I wanted to. As well as our drama club directors, Micki and Melanie, again two women that I looked up to and needed in my life at those moments.

I remember being 16 and looking forward to a particular solo I had at the choir concert. I worked on manifesting this particular solo for the whole year, before this moment, and I remember it being one of the things I'd spend a lot of after-school hours on.

When it was my senior year and I finally got the opportunity to perform the solo I had been working on, I was so excited. I would spend hours in my room locked up, repeatedly rehearsing, just to get everything as flawless today as it could be. I never thought of it as making my parents proud as most children like me at the concert did, I never even thought my mother would come. I just wanted to do something for myself, something to make me feel the least bit special.

I still vividly remember rounding up on the final day, all dressed and ready to go. Just as I had walked into the kitchen to see who was around at the time to inform them that it was almost time to go, I found my mother at the table with a huge glass of water and a huge bottle of pills.

She had overdosed.

I was in such a frenzy as I was 16 and didn't know what to do. I remember seeing her pupils dilated and her skin very pale. I was so afraid and my stomach felt stuffy ~ I felt like I was going to throw up.

My first thought was to call my uncle which I did, and he got to the scene as fast as he could. When he got there, he made the call to 911, and she was taken to the hospital shortly after that. I froze to the ground with several questions on my mind at the time.

"How was I going to perform this solo now?", I thought to myself. With all of this on my mind, there was no way that I could perform the song anymore. But, the show must go on, and I did. I performed. I kept it a secret. No one knew what was going on in my home, or what had gone on in my home at that time.

The rush of performing didn't last forever, soon I started to associate performance with this trauma. Soon, the scare grew into something larger, and gradually but eventually robbed me of my talent and passion for music, for performing in theater.

I stopped playing the guitar for so long after this incident that I forgot how to, and I stopped singing publicly. I completely stopped performing in theaters and I gradually forgot how to enjoy singing before people, even at karaoke with friends.

Music, the source of my joy for extended periods before this incident, now validated pain and trauma. That scene of seeing my mother lying lifelessly beside a glass of water and a bottle emptied of pills gave me a hard time dreaming at night. But it put out my dreams of ever performing in public for a long time after I graduated that year.

And then she persisted.

5

My Mother got remarried when I was in 4th grade to a White man. Again, still in my home having the feeling of no one looking like me. Ok, so no one looked like me. My thoughts at the forefront were that the abuse of my sister and I may finally come to an end.

We were also quite fancying the idea of having a brother who would now be our protector. Not only did we gain a brother from the marriage, but we got two of them.

However, we were wrong about the abuse possibly ending. It never stopped.

If anything, my mother showed us just how hurtful verbal abuse can be when compared with physical abuse. Verbal abuse hurts in so many more ways than physical abuse can even dare to prick. We were not getting protected by anybody as well.

Although our stepfather himself never hit us, he never stopped my mother from hitting us whenever she could. Failure to protect. I gained a stepfather that was not protective and stepbrothers that did things to their stepsister that should never be done. The only advantage we saw from the marriage was the fact that the mother didn't have to shoulder all the responsibilities like she used to. At this point, the majority of us living with her were already trying to earn money to cater to our extensive needs and basic wants. It just gave us more time to ourselves outdoors.

It was during this collision course that I met my first boyfriend, which was my first romantic experience. I was a sophomore in high school when I met him. He was in his final year, and we met through a friend of ours who was in the Drama club at the time. We had an instant connection.

I remember him being amazing at playing the guitar, and since I had a thing for music at this point, I thought we'd make a great pair. Also, he had long hair which just seemed to fuel my fascination for him, for reasons I do not understand to this day. Actually I do, I loved long hair. It was enough to make any teenage girl go crazy. A guitar player, with long hair, who had an amazing personality. We started dating, and we were together for about two and a half years.

I was 16 years old at the time, and he was one of the nicest, kindest people I had come to know, especially during this period of my life when I was going through a lot physically, mentally, and psychologically. He made me feel safe. He probably didn't understand that at that time in my life, he was saving me and my whole soul.

We had quite the adventure together, and I chose to follow him because I had always reacted to find myself and I was really curious about who I was at this point in my life. He knew the majority of what was going on with me at home, and I would go to his place often as soon as we started dating. He would come to me occasionally as well. I had technically met him when I was 15 and wanted to get together then, but interestingly enough, my mother would not let me then. The moment I got the ok, he was on speed dial. My Mother didn't perhaps bat an eye to our relationship, and how it was, especially since I was at such a young age because she had started to date and had gotten married quite early herself. I mean I was 16. However, his parents always looked happy to see me. This made us spend most of our time at his house and a little less at mine. Again, feeling safe, and in love.

Although we didn't have any music classes together, he taught me some of the few strings that I could play on the guitar at the time. Introduced me to new music. We would go to carnivals together, or the coffee shop, fishing, hanging out, whatever it may be. I just wanted to spend every waking moment with him. So I did. We were just a regular teenage couple at the time. I remember even trying to smoke weed with him for the first time. Following him on the adventure.

He was the first person I was fully intimate with, my first love. This particular phase of my life came hurriedly like a whirlwind, and I feel that it left just about how it came. One certain day, after overthinking things like I normally did, I knew that he was not going to be my forever and that was that. We broke up shortly after that, and I never regret the decision to this day. Although he was a nice, genuine guy, I was searching for something more for me. I do think about how I may have hurt him with this rationale. I was searching for someone who I would get to spend the rest of my life with, and it wasn't long after this that I found my husband Matt.

After I broke up with him, we kept in touch for a short time, until we didn't. However, it wasn't long after I ended things with him that I started going out with Matt. I was not fully over him that quickly, you do not just delete your first love, your first everything from your life, and never think about them again.

As for Matthew, I had known him a few years before I began to see him as a potential love interest, and a while before we got engaged and eventually married.

When I was 12, I used to go to a Christian youth group on Wednesdays. This was one of the few outlets I chose to use in letting out the pressure of my mother's abuse on me, and it was easily one of the safest places to escape. There, I became quite close with the youth pastor Craig as he was always willing to listen to me speak about my problems without thinking of shutting me off for a change, and he slowly became a father figure to me as time flew by. Little did I know then, that Matthew, his son, would be my future husband.

Matt had messaged me after I had just stepped out of my first relationship to ask me if I was willing to hang out with him. At this time, my best friend Tawny was dating Matt's brother and she had already egged our relationship on right from the very start. She thought we would be a perfect fit.

Shortly after we connected as per his request, a message on Myspace started it all, we ended up going on a date and felt a mutual understanding like we had known each other for millennia. We started dating almost immediately after that.

Our relationship was just as quick as the whirlwind event from my previous boyfriend but was quite different from it in the sense that the feeling was incomparable. With Matt, it felt like we were two teenagers who looked young, but knew what they were doing. This must have been why I didn't hesitate to agree to marry him when he asked me to, despite me being 19 years old at the time, and Matt being 24.

And then she persisted.

6

We moved to California as soon as we got married towards the end of the year 2008, and I reckon we were residents in this place till the year 2011.

As newlyweds who were barely settling into life as a couple, into the complexities of independence and the responsibilities that come with creating and heading home, Matt and I fought to find our place in the small city we chose to reside in, in California, doing everything we possibly could to enjoy our first few years of conjugal bliss as we explored this reality. In search of jobs in this unfamiliar environment, Matt landed a job at a nearby gas station working as a mechanic and I got a job at a Ski resort mountain alternatively. The goal was to not have a goal or intention, just live our lives to the fullest and love every bit of it, which we did in what was considerably "grand style".

We partied as we had never done before, made friends spontaneously and especially without being selective of them, and we would ski together, having fun without a care in the world. It was a boisterous, racy, and relatively reckless way of life, as the effects of being party animals soon, took a toll on us as we further continued in its mediocrity. We lived the life of spendthrifts, like teenagers who just landed their first job in the three figures, and had no sense of responsibility or belonging whatsoever. We lived from paycheck to paycheck.

One of the most important Pros of these three years in California was the opportunity we got as a couple to be able to understand each other on a fundamental and dynamic level, without the interference of anybody else (be them childhood friends or family members at least from my side), due to the estrangement period. We were able to achieve bonding with each other, on a level that most newly wedded couples around us marveled at, and it increased the level of connection we now have and nurture, and have learned to groom over the years. Those times were bittersweet for us and filled with a lot of education for us to take home.

After a while, we became fed up with living life like that. Of spending what we ate as we made it, and not having any savings or plans for the future for ourselves and our children. It appeared as though we had lost track of our desires for the distinct and peculiar dreams we had both talked about and shared before we got married, and it was almost like we were losing our way with each passing day. This train of thought grew especially worse during times when we couldn't eat or take care of some basic responsibilities at home because we couldn't save whatever money we were spending. This was when we both decided to stop being wasteful and unintentional with our money, and start saving or investing in the glory of its future. It was only after an agreement by the both of us to do this, however, and an intentional approach to all our financial-related dealings, that we were able to curb the vice once and for all, and we no longer went to those types of parties or skiing exercises. It was probably the first huge step we took intentionally, and it was the first of many.

Excluding that, however, we still went on several vacations to the beach or some of California's best, and we would hang out like we were still just boyfriend and girlfriend, and not even like we were married folks.

What this did for us, this three-year period away from family alone on our own, was to bind us together in ways that went beyond just the fundamentals, and it made us understand each other and grew more affinity for each other as time passed.

Most times, I would get asked questions around the essence of marital bliss or the key ingredients to Marital longevity, and my answer every time would be understanding to a depth that cannot be fathomed talk less 'breached', and I always attribute this to the story of my husband and me, especially around the events of these three years.

When Matt and I first got to know each other as we had just gotten married and were still just working out the romance, we would not solve our problems or internal strife by talking about it, but by pretending it didn't happen at all. We were young, and had gotten engaged eight short months after we started dating. This is the most common reaction for couples who have just gotten married, as they would try to swallow their reservations about each other, in a bid to tolerate one another till they're concerns or worries reach a breaking point and explode app over the place in heavy arguments, lovers quarrels or fights. To make it even more particular, this is common with young couples, and Matt and I were young at the time we got married and moved to California. I was around 19 and aged to 21 then which just defines us as babies who had gotten married, and we could have been susceptible to these kinds of mistakes considering our experiences and young age overall.

You would also note that my first boyfriend was the only other person I was with serious with until I got married, and there wasn't much room for comparison with somebody else or any particular pool of expertise and experience in relationships, so I didn't have much to go by in terms of understanding shortcomings or oversights on my part or my husbands part, and this could have been the source of a series of problems in our marriage if the three year period at California didn't happen.

Probably because of our time in California alone, or because we took out the first periods of our lives together to be alone and fully understand each other, Matt and I formed a union that never fought in the course of their marriage. Matt and I have never fought about anything since we got married.

Now don't get me wrong, we have had disputes, arguments, little stifles, and verbal disagreements which are normal and common for most marriages if not all of them, but we have never gotten to the point where we felt it couldn't be settled between us, or where there was an incident of him being physical on me and anything closely related to those kinds of things.

We never had anything close to an aggressive quarrel because we understand each other to an almost telepathic level, and we have been through a lot together on our own, that we cannot be swayed by circumstances or any sort of situation, no matter how terrible it might appear to be at first. We have evolved through the years as this kind of symbiotic organisms fused as one by a very deep sense of trust and understanding (like lichens for instance), and I think that this is what makes couples, irrespective of their age, create a marital union that could work for them. This is the only thing that could make any marriage stand the test of time, and come out unscathed eventually.

To be analogically specific, I would describe marriage as a mutual agreement between multiple persons, who have decided to build a sand castle of their own by a preferred seashore or riverbank of their choice. As they struggle to build it together, to understand each of their roles in raising appropriately, each of the different important aspects of this sand castle to make it as sturdy and as lasting as possible, they first need to build it with such dexterity, that it is strong enough to withstand the sea winds that would eventually come down heavily on their castle in a really short time. Also, they have to be careful to not get in each other's way as they try to raise the building so as not to accidentally collapse it because this could happen especially with younger couples who have not yet learned or understood what to do, and how to do it with a precise amount of hard work and consideration for their partner.

Finally, whatever building they end up raising together must be sturdy enough to withstand the river tides from the river banks, that break through their normal limit and sell to destroy any sandcastles on its shore that were not built with enough durability or dexterity by their makers. For one, these sandcastles are akin to the nature of the relationship between couples in general, and these scenarios chiefly represent the diverse number of issues that could destroy this relationship and in turn kill the marriage, if it isn't raised sturdy enough to stand the test of time.

This in turn physically represents itself as the numerous challenges that couples in a marital union are prone to face daily, and it is evident how sturdy they have built their sandcastle, which would determine if they could stand the test of time when these situations arise. The situations are always constant, and cannot be avoided especially if folx have decided to be together.

And then she persisted.

7

When Matthew was younger, about 12 years old or thereabout, he got sick and had to be taken to the hospital. He was never really the kind of child that experienced difficulties with his health growing up, but he suddenly started to feel extreme levels of pain in his stomach at irregular intervals that were disconcerting to his parents. For that reason, they decided to see what was wrong in a hospital not too far from their residence in Michigan.

Upon getting there, they were told that he had massive intestinal complications, that about 22½ feet of his intestines were gangrenous, and had to be expelled from his body for him to at least survive and return to normalcy. He had surgery specifically for this purpose.

However, a few years after we had gotten married and were in California, this series of stomach pains and belly aches resurfaced again, and it was not until ten years still later, that and he was diagnosed with Crohn's disease, by another specialist doctor back in Michigan. He had to be taken there for us to fully grasp the extent to which he was hurting or sick.

After this diagnosis and some prescriptions alongside guidelines were instructed to him, we began walking together on a path that saw him take care of his health the best, daily. We had to watch what he ate, what he drank, and the likes, and carefully pick out and rearrange his diet to suit his condition, while we hoped and prayed for his speedy recovery. This all started to happened sometime during our three-year stay in California.

Additionally, I also had problems of my own that I faced, during these three years in California. I worked at a ski resort mountain for most of the time, and as such had the opportunity to snowboard with my husband and friends whenever I wanted to, solely because of the nature of my job here. I truly enjoyed snowboarding, as it was not just a therapeutic experience for me but was also really enjoyable, and I found myself getting to love doing it, with each passing day I was opportune to work there.

I had just started getting good at it then, and I would sometimes snowboard solo or go with friends and sometimes alongside my husband, and we would just have the most fun we could snowboard all day, without a care in the world.

On one of these times, however, I was snowboarding and I fell in the mountains and broke my shoulder in the process. It was a terrifying and excruciatingly painful experience, and I had to have surgery on the shoulder to fix the possible lacerations, dislocations, and separations that might have happened during the fall because it did feel like a couple of those had happened during the fall, and I vividly remember the unbearable pain I was in at the time.

Now, after each of these individual situations that happened to my husband and me during our time in California, we were always there for each other in these times and stuck with each other to be the necessary mental and physical aid we both needed, especially when we could not do some particular activities that we generally used to, and this was the building block or better yet stepping stone, for elevation to a higher, greater level on understanding in our marriage.

Unions such as these, lifetime unions, will always birth several kinds of challenges and problems.

Just as gold has to pass through a really hot furnace to be refined and to glitter its worth without necessarily magnifying its already evident quality, marriages that several young couples cover, admire, and seek to have, have all experienced different types and kinds of problems that have tested their loyalty and commitment to each other, in ways they cannot see from the outside. Practically speaking, it is how well couples successfully overcome crises that determine how long they would last, till their next series of challenges comes about to ravage them in that manner.

Marriages that last aren't magically created. It's not really about sexual compatibility, financial comfort or any other mundane thing that people think keeps marriages these days, but first of an understanding that is beyond the physical, and then of persistence that is encompassing, and that seeks to rise above any challenge, no matter how colossal it may seem at the time of its arrival.

Partners must always bear in mind, that they plan to age together, and with age comes not just the inability to no longer be the person they once were physically, mentally, and otherwise due to nature's fundamental effects on the very fiber of life, but also with the required maturity that is acquired and activated, after each of these couples overcome each of these difficulty levels that life throws at them, in this rollercoaster game of 'dare to do that they are continually faced with, as time goes by. I am not the same person now in my mid thirtys, that I was when I was nineteen.

However, with each difficulty they surpass, and with each barrier they break, couples should always remember that they have by-so-doing, acquired a newfound level of growth and understanding, that they would normally not have had if they were not faced with these challenges going forth.

The progress made by a marital union can be akin to a game of bluff, where the only way to truly win is to persist through the trying times no matter what and never give up. This is because the most important ingredient of a successful and lasting marriage, is persistence and trust in each other, beyond every single 'Union threatening" scenario, that life throws at you on the journey.

And then she persisted.

8

Immediately after I got married to Matt and we elected to move away from Michigan, far away from my mother's grasp, what I refer to as the practice 'estrangement' period began.

Matthew was a huge fan of the idea, especially knowing the kind of person my mother was, and he agreed with me that it would be illogical of us to want to raise our children in front of a person who isn't even a role model to her children. After we moved, I never got to see my mother again for a long time. In years.

Living with Matt across the county was one of the best periods of my life and it sort of replaced most of the bad memories I have growing up with some really good ones. This makes life worth living, and I'm so happy and thankful every day for having made me meet and get to marry such a wonderful person. His family is extremely supportive as well.

With Matt, I was able to focus more on my career and attempt to find my path and purpose in life. I discovered that I had a passion for child welfare.

It could have been because I always wanted to be rescued from the hellish situation that I was put through while living with my mother, but I grew fond of children's rights because of my history as a victim of child abuse and domestic violence. It was in getting a degree in psychology that I began to realize some of the ills my mother had done to us, to me, in the name of parenting.

It became even weirder to me that nobody in my family, or in that neighborhood in Michigan where I grew up reported my mother's abuse to children's protection services. I wanted to become a beacon of hope to children like me who have nobody to stand up for them in the face of abuse and aggressive behaviors of any scale. This became my purpose and mission.

It was one of the reasons I took college more seriously than I had ever previously done, and worked hard to earn the degree and more others after this.

It was also around this period that I took in my first son Victor. I became a mom.

Tawny also continued to stand by me , and continues to this day to be my best childhood friend. She was always a huge fan of me and my work and still is, and is usually always there to support my progress and positivity, but never also hesitated to give me an earful anytime I was going down the wrong path or letting the depression get to me. She reminds me of the wonderful wife, mother, and leader that I am, and makes me feel confident about myself in social cycles, at work, and as a woman in the 21st-century modern day and age.

During the period of my estrangement from home, as I grew to love and accept more friends and family, my maternal extended family suffered huge blows in my absence.

Firstly, my grandmother died. She had been quite aged, but she was always the mother of the whole family, and she was one of the only reasons why most of the members of my mother's maternal family stayed close together in Michigan. Without her influence, they would have all left decades ago as it wasn't so difficult to see the differences they shared and their effects on their relationship and communication. If everything was going alright with them, maybe my mother would have confided in any of them as to what was going on with her and would have probably not tried to kill herself.

Excluding my grandmother, the second loss hit closer to home than I could have expected. My mother's husband from remarriage and my stepfather also passed away.

This particular loss was of more severity to me than my grandmother's, and I was told the mornings for him went on for extended periods as my family was trying to deal with the shock.

I could not bring myself to attend any of their burials or funeral processions. I felt that the precedent of seeing my mother at such a time when I was still undergoing therapy and recovering, was not the best thing for my mental health. Other members of my family didn't see it the way I did, and labeled me a selfish and despicable woman.

The truth is, I did want to go. I would have loved to attend their funerals, and pay my last respects to them both, as they were both important family members to me irrespective of what they had and had not done. They were still family, no matter what.

However, I could not go because I felt it would straighten my 'already scalded and just repairing' mental health, and my therapist confirmed these fears of mine.

I did NOT go because the cons outweigh the pros at the time, and I have never regretted that decision to this day. I do have my grandmothers ashes in my closet.

This period of estrangement, of not talking to my mother or anybody directly related to her on my maternal side, lasted for about 10 years.

And then she persisted.

9

One of the major reasons I was able to stay apart from my mother for 10 years, go through a mental and psychological healing process, and get back on my feet strong enough to forgive my mother eventually was primarily because of the support from my husband and his side of the family, and my therapy sessions with Lauren.

When she felt I had recovered enough and it was time, Lauren had me slowly think about reconciling with what my mother would look like. I had no reason not to think about this at all, at this point, because I could see the changes in her therapy sessions quite evidently in my everyday life. The thought of reconciliation with my mother had crossed my mind.

First off, I was slowly becoming the outspoken ~ extroverted woman that I once was when I was still just a girl. I easily welcomed and managed leadership positions, and I slowly started to get over my fear of performing in public that I had developed after my mother's suicide scare.

Also, I now began to smile more, and mean it, more than I had ever done for that period than in 5 years before that. I was changing, growing to become a better person and there were signs that my persistence was finally paying off. It was a truly beautiful thing.

After all this time, the time came to see her. When I saw her, I could see that she had aged a lot. Her skin had gotten more sullen, blue, and she now had visible strands of gray hair on her head, like her hair had turned white completely.

We talked for a few minutes, and I could say that this was the most surface-level conversation I ever remember having with her. After that call, I still to this day have not had a verbal conversation with her again. During my therapy sessions with Lauren, I always talked about the wandering of my paternal side of the family. I spoke of our deeper connections during one of our sessions and suggested that I track down my Black origin better, especially now that I was an adult, to see exactly what I would find from the search. She wanted me to still ask my mother about all these things and just test the waters to have an inkling of an idea as to what happened to my paternal relatives, and she was baffled by the idea that my mother claimed all my father's relatives were dead.

She thought there should be at least one left from the larger extended family at least, and I thought this made sense too, to be honest. And so I set out to ask my mother about my father's family, again.

When I was a child, say 13 or 14, I asked my mother about my father and what had happened with his family. I always knew that my father had passed away when I was 13. She had told me that my father's family had passed away shortly after. Always very adamant that both my paternal grandmother and aunt had passed away as well. She never made mention of the cause of their deaths and I had always thought that this was because she didn't know at the time. It made sense to me then because apparently, she always claimed my father left her pregnant after he had physically abused her and no member of his family had attempted to visit her till she raised the child all on her own. I thought this to be a possibility, given the circumstances she had explained.

However, when I saw her in 2022, what she told me was quite different from what I remember her saying to me about my father and his side of the family as a child. This time, she told me that my grandmother had passed away a few years ago and that my aunt had been hit by a train. The sudden change in description and its obvious discrepancies caused me to suspect that a few things were wrong with what she had said. It was at this point that I sought out my father's relatives wherever they might have been, even if it was just one of them as Lauren had said. I searched online for our family tree on this mobile application that apparently can and it took a few days, but I found what I thought was a lead to locating them.

I received a call and spoke on the phone to an aged woman who was so welcoming and elated to see me. It didn't take long on the call for me to discover that she was my father's direct mother, my grandmother who my mother had claimed was dead on several occasions. I set out to meet them.

I discovered a whole new branch of family members on my father's side that I never knew or thought I would ever have. I went from having no paternal family to a really warm and welcoming family on that side in a flash. I was for the first time affiliated with the Black art of my family and could finally begin to explore my link and relationship with my Black origin, descent, and culture.

My grandmother also divulged to me that my father didn't pass away in quite the manner that was divulged to me.

He had passed away from AIDS in 2001, which when matched with my history, was around the time I was 13 years old.

After that call, I learned of family reunions that happen yearly and I was always welcome to join. I set out to plan a trip 2023 in anticipation to meet my extended family This discovery created a deep-seated realization of myself as a true biracial woman, and it was only then that I felt the nostalgia of both worlds and not the 'White girl in a biracial skin' reservation that I had subconsciously had in me till this time.

I had a whole family. Hundreds of family members that I had known nothing about. People who looked like me. I spent the whole weekend with them, and I felt like I belonged.

And then she persisted.

10

Whenever it concerned my education and learning, I always did the best I could at school. It must have started from believing that getting good grades was one of the surefire ways of getting as far away from my mother as possible whilst also having the power to stand for myself, and I always overworked myself when it came to tests or promotional exams in high school and then college.

When I got to college, I was interested in a variety of things, and I tried as much as I possibly could to dabble in most of these things and get a degree in them. This must have been why I was able to curate my interest in psychology and sociology as I always wanted to study the human mind and its desired communication systems, whilst also picking up a bachelor's and master's degree in Psychology while I schooled in California at the time.

I was interested in the human psyche, and in human behavior, primarily because I was always curious to know why my mother was always angry, and if there was anything I could do to quell her anger and make us a better family. I also wanted to be the end of the generational abuse that seemed to be dominantly present on my mother's side of the family as I wanted my kids to have no path in the abuse and trauma I had gone through before I even dreamt of getting married or had met Matt.

While I studied this in California, I had so much fun and I put my mind to it so much that I never had a failing grade. This might have been because I had a passion for either course and had none of the few factors that distract teenagers my age from school.

After my college education, I needed to find a job. I was no stranger to working as I started my first job as a 14-year-old, and I had a clear vision of exactly what it wanted to be like.

Immediately I got a job at the child welfare agency I had applied for, I was only too joyous to receive the offer. There, I made it a personal goal to work as hard as I could, to get as far as I could in this aspect of work, to achieve my dreams of being the best Adoption Professional that I could be, and I ensured that all kids like me who had difficulty growing up due to psychological or physical trauma of any kind. I so badly wanted to be elevate the voices of those with lived experience.

In working with these children that experienced abused and abusive homes, I discovered from the statistics that a majority of children who are abused before the age of 16 are almost always Brown or Black kids, and it was my mission to put forth all of the efforts in my work to advocate for these children who looked like me.

Once getting the opportunity to work with the kids for a while, I discovered a striking similarity between the abuse they faced and mine, and how most of them were always of the racially Black population. Why were the Black families being ripped and torn apart?

My role was to ensure that if the child could not stay with their families, that they were able to be moved with other family that would keep them safe, unlike my mother who was not afforded this help, nor did folx know what was behind our closed doors, and that these children never get to face the extent of psychological trauma and pressure that I faced and that could spiral their life out of control.

As I worked in the child welfare sector for about eight years from when I first got the job, I discovered that I was getting moved through positions of different authorities within the institution, and this greatly helped to broaden my study scope as time passed.

From foster care, to recruitment, to licensing, I was not just getting moved around various offices but was also getting greater roles and responsibilities to shoulder with each passing stage that passed and office I acquired. Eventually, I was given a position of a lifetime as an Adoption Trainer. Something that I had dreamed about for years.

I used my position as a supervisor, to make certain moves and changes as effective as I could make them, and I created the most precedent I could for the care of all children of color so that no child might have to suffer from child abuse or the prolonged effects of parental racial aggressions, ever again.

And then she persisted.

11

In the year 2020, I got the opportunity to be an adoption trainer for the state, and to be able to train new workers that were just as excited about starting in this sector of work, as I was when I first started. I am so passionate about Adoption, that all I envisioned was transferring my knowledge to others in a positive light.

It was a desire of mine to give aid and road maps to all these new workers to help them give the children deserving of these needs, and I was more than happy to jump at the opportunity to do so when it presented itself to me.

This opportunity also created the precedent to change my trajectory as a person in life, and it gave me the ability to see most of my dreams come true on a rather personal level, even far more than I could have ever hoped or imagined for.

While beginning in the training department, I remember having a worthwhile conversation with a supervisor on the very first day, who had the burning desire to touch on the areas of racism in our realm of work and study, and he ran the idea by me to see what I thought about it. He said to me "Let's talk about race!" I responded, " We can do that, can we have this conversation ongoing?" I couldn't help but be in awe of his willingness to want me to have these conversations.

I was committing at that moment to doing all of the deeper research to uncover the ills of systemic racism in the child welfare system and do everything in my power to work toward the dismantling of it. I was willing to commit 100% of my time and energy to the projects regarding the work as soon as I heard of them. Anti-racism work was now at forefront and I worked very hard to make sure that our voice and mandate is heard by as many folx in the child welfare sector as possible on many different levels of the state.

For this to be possible, however, for me to give a voice to the Black and Brown children who are experiencing the system and who were living their lives every day under the practical effects of this societal menace, I had to first understand my origin in Black culture and heritage. I decided it was time for me to immerse myself into Black culture fully to properly understand myself and work on my own racial identity to the fullest.

I know now that I am not a person who has experience inside the foster care or adoption system, as I was not removed, despite numerous precognitions and beliefs that I had about this as a child due to the extent of abuse and trauma I faced with my biological mother. However, I always felt and still feel this semblance, a similarity of sorts, whenever I talk or work with the interaracially adopted kids who have a similar story of racial aggressions, anthological trauma injuries, and scars. They always talk about this characteristic treatment that they were made to face characteristics, at school, in church, or generally at social gatherings, and these things have driven them to the edge and have sought to lay waste to their dreams and desires, just as it had threatened to do with mine which is probably why I always feel a sense of camaraderie whenever I see children like this, in need of this type of help. In my case, I was always made to feel like this segregated half-caste was not desired by her society because I was biracial and didn't know where I belonged. It was a horrible feeling.

I would get told that I'm a Black person with White person privileges, that I had people that loved me because I was Black and/or White (even if these were not), and that such unions could not happen without the most delicate of romantic feelings and inseparable attractions coming into play and I always felt terrible hearing them as a child. People would look at me and say things like; "you talk like a White girl, you're smart for a Black girl or you're pretty for a Black girl", and these things done intentionally or unintentionally would always remind me and kids like me (as I'd later learned) that we were this different creature or human being from the rest of the world which was always an extra weight or addition to the identity crisis we were already facing especially for a person like me who didn't know her father growing up.

Some of them would be done as compliments and could seem practically harmless to the offender. Statements like "of course you're fast, you're the best of both worlds after all", or stroking my hair and making certain comments like "your hair looks so nice! Must be good to be Black and White", and all these other passive statements that could be made by our teachers, or a classmate, or even that random stranger by the side of the road that you somehow get to see everyday as you return from school. Most of the time, I didn't even know it was a microaggressive statement, and I never knew the right words to respond with because I didn't have anybody to talk to about it who understood exactly what I was going through and could give me the right answers to all these microaggressive statements that slowly caused psychological injuries within me that took time to heal.

This was important to be the fullest ally and activist to stand in front of several persons of different races and ethnicities share my story with them and to tell them of racism, the dangers of the White supremacy thought train and the need for equity of rights for our LGBTQIA+ communities. It was during this period that I applied to be a part of the Minority Professional Leadership Development Program hosted by the National Children's Bureau and AdoptUSKids. I was selected nationally among 15 other people for this honor. It was at this program, that the speaking platform I had been looking for to reach out to as many people as possible was made available for me.

The program helped me connect with a wealth of people and organizations, and gave me a platform to be able to help people, and as such help myself as a result.

Not only did it give me the chance to establish my own identity, but, it also created an opportunity for me to do what I love in public speaking, content writing, and educating others on child welfare and dismantling systemic racism.

Around this same time, I also got the opportunity to join forces with Detroit Moms.

The Detroit Moms is a organization that acts as a coalition union for women of Detroit. As a majority of their population was and is ,White women, I used the opportunity to educate these women on the roles of mothers in dismantling racism generally in the U.S, and connect with other moms who look like me, and have similar trials and tribulations as myself.

When I speak to these mothers, through social media, podcasting, and writing, and I feel the responsibility and need to let them understand the importance of educating their kids and their neighbors' kids on racism, racial aggressions, and how to avoid doing these things that hurt people of color around them in their speech and their relations with them.

I let them understand, that one of the major ways in which people of color are dealt an unfair hand by their friends and family who constitute the society is through the deprecating act of feigning "color blindness" when relating to people of color in a bid to avoid being racist, and this does not make matters any better or make the offender any different from a potential racist.

People should be *Color Brave*, and thus children should be taught the need and optimal ways to see people of color and appreciate them as just human beings, rather than pretend to not see this and end up being insensitive to them as a result. Recognizing their oppression. Children do see color as a negative most times even better than adults, and if taught the proper ways to address this difference could be the key to the desired future of equality and color balance that the world needs and has been striving for, for centuries of its existence.

I always let parents know, that *"what could be microaggression to one individual and seem like no big deal for them could be macro aggressive to another individual elsewhere with the same specifications, and could drive them to the verge of despair, delirium and suicidal thoughts or even actions"*.

I thus have stood another interest in consultation and advocacy and used the opportunity to talk to these women about the rising roles of a mother in parenting a great social justice warrior, and the responsibility that rests on our shoulders through this set precedent.

This was one of the few and most memorable events that saw me evolve into the version of myself that I am today, which I consider the best with a lot of extra room for growth. I was a mom, a wife, a good person, and an advocate for justice.

And then she persisted.

12

About 12 years ago, just before the estrangement period, I decided to set a boundary between my mother and me.

It began when I was in labor with my first son Victor and was taken to the hospital to have him. My mother, my sister, and my husband's family, at the time, were informed about this, and they all came to see me, including my mother.

When she arrived, my mother began making everything about her without caring for any other person's feelings at the time, and I made the decision not to let her into the delivery room to see me and be with me as I was delivering this baby. I did not feel this bond with my mother and did not want her in there at this time. She threw a huge fit in the hospital that was extremely embarrassing to everybody present and cted the unnecessary attention of the medical staff.

After I heard about this incident, I went into deep thought, and finally settled on the idea of estranging my mother from me or any of my affairs for the time being. This was the only way for me to be away from her and the negative aura that she exuded or would bring to me and my recovering mental state of health at the time. I also felt she would be a terrible influence on my children, and felt it best to not let them have anything to do with her. This was what was best for me and for the kind of mother that I envisioned myself to be from the not-so-distant past of my life, for the productive and peaceful life that I wanted for me and my kids in the future.

This was actually how the estrangement started. This did not happen immediately at that moment, it took some time as we continued to have these persistent moments of triggering trauma. When Victor was about 6 months old is when the estrangement started, as I never spoke with my mother from that day onward and it remained that way for almost ten years. The loss of contact was important to my recovery from the psychological injuries that my mother had given me, and I knew that it was only right to not talk to her till I had completely gotten rid of the trauma indents in my brain and was able to live without that depression or anxiety resonating back again. I battled PTSD for a long time, because of my mother's abusive nature.

Now despite choosing to not be in contact with my mother for this extended period that almost got to 10 years. I had a indirect way of checking up on her, and I knew almost everything that was going on with her during this time. I kept in touch with my sister who was still in touch with her during that period and was my informant on all situations regarding my mother. She told me all I needed to know about her whenever I asked, and I was satisfied with what I knew about her at that moment, for the time being. I wouldn't have wanted to know more, even if I was getting paid for it.

I remember a lot of people who heard about the state of my relationship with my mother at the time, tell me to reconcile with her and just abruptly forgive her whilst overlooking what she had done. They would say things like "We don't get to choose our parents", or "We only get to live once with one family", or even "Your mother would always be your mother, despite who she is and what she has done". I always shuddered when I heard these words.

To me, I had no mother. My mother simply and only gave birth to me, but she never stood in for me as mental support or moral confidant throughout my stay with her and I can barely recollect any fond or happy memories I had with her, no matter how long I try to reminisce. There may have been some good ones to be fair, but the history of the bad ones is so many that they suppress and shroud the memory of any good ones I could have possibly remembered. My mother never acted like a mother, and so that train of thought to me was always invalid. Those could only work for mothers who, at one point or the other in time, tried to be good parents to their kids.

Even now when I think about it, I still believe that it wasn't completely her fault. There was a history of generational abuse and trauma from my mother's family that her mother must have passed down to her through several beatings like the ones she inflicted on us while we were growing up, but I always decided that I would be the end to that cycle and break it.

That I would choose not to continue on to my children just as my mother had done.

That I would be different.

Now, I am different as a better woman, a better wife to my husband,

and a better mother to my kids.

Now, I have lived through the pain with persistence and I know I made the right choice. As humans, we always have a choice.

And then she persisted

13

When I was pregnant with Victor; my first son, I experienced all sorts of prejudice and unfairness I had always thought to be fables or myths, whenever I had come to see such news on on the television. It was not just a show of subtle racial practices and racial aggressions, but it got to a developed stage of oversight and inconsiderate treatment, and some of those things really threatened my life and the life of my son Victor as well, and this just goes to show how deeply seated these issues are and affect us in our society.

I began to notice the changes when I was first pregnant with him, around the second to the third trimester of the period before I was to give birth. I had persistent headaches that wouldn't stop without pain reliefs, or their stronger counterparts in active ingredients and dosage, *pain killers*, and my husband I agreed to go see a doctor check what exactly was causing these. It wasn't even just the headaches or to be precise *migraines*, but the way they were affecting my vision, speech, and taste, and the way they rendered me practically unable to do even as much as lift a finger. I could not see at all.

I remember the head pangs being as severe and debilitating as I had ever experienced or could ever imagine, and I had no idea people could hurt like that and still be fine eventually. We were severely worried at the time, and I was always distressed, to a level where it got difficult to sleep.

At the hospital, the doctor who attended to me told me what I was feeling was normal, and was probably because it was my first issue, and that this was my body reacting to all the strange things that were happening to me. I found it hard to believe that.

I requested stronger doses of painkillers to help reduce the pain as it was becoming unbearable, but the doctor refused and glossed over my requests like it was nothing important. I want to preface, I understand I could not take more than tylenol while being pregnant, but there had to be relief. To be precise, he told me to *"bear with it"* and that it would *"all soon be over in a couple of months.* I was extremely infuriated by his months and attitude, but there was little to nothing I could do at the time since he was the gynecologist I had been with since the start of the antenatal period of this particular pregnancy. I felt like going to another gynecologist at that point might complicate issues further, and I decided to endure and stay till it was all over. In truth, it was my first experience, and I was both young and not knowledgeable enough about some things to have made the right decision about going into the third trimester. I had gone for my routine antenatal checkup one day and was told that my blood pressure was high. This was not only dangerous to me as a person but as a pregnant woman, as it was equally that dangerous to my unborn son, if not much worse. The doctors felt it would be best at that point for me to have the baby a little ahead of schedule, and my husband and I agreed to it since we were assured that this was what was best for safe delivery. After that, a day was chosen and labor was induced, and I went into labor on that particular day.

During the labor, I felt a lot of things were wrong with my body and I freaked out ~ a lot. I still feel this was normal since it was my first issue, and the least the nurses could do was to assure and reassure me that everything was going to be alright by providing me with what was possible at the time, and gently telling me that it wouldn't be good for me if what I requested was not relevant or worse still, harmful to my present state at the time. The staff however outrightly ignored me like I was demented or hallucinating, and none of my requests were listened to, talk more granted. My husband and Mother in law were in the room with me, but it was our first baby, we didn't really know what was going on.

To make matters worse, my epidural wasn't working, and it was so evident that it made me worried and nearly have panic attacks.

I was in labor for about one and a half days, 33 hours to be precise, and I was treated like I was not susceptible to pain, just because I was Black or something.

Because of the way he was born, after the labor had passed and I had been successfully stabilized and cleared to go home, the doctors then said Victor had a fever and couldn't go home otherwise it would be dangerous and could affect his health. We had to stay a couple of days extra, and he was given antibiotics for this period before his temperature normalized, and he was finally able to come home with us.

In retrospect, there is this uncanny, poorly birthed belief (I would rather refer to it as a myth though) about Black women in hospitals, especially during pregnancies or labor, or in the postnatal stages of this. I have heard it from the mouths of a few friends, seen it voiced out from the lips of Black women that I know just neighbors or colleagues, and others like me, just feelings like it was just another belief based on falsehood at the time. I didn't agree with it, till I experienced it firsthand, and had no other choice but to protest against the injustice and prejudice I had seen happen right before my eyes.

This narrative states that Black-skinned women are impervious to pain, or are not susceptible to pain the way other races are. It is a wrong notion to have, and it has cost women in hospitals, especially during childbirth, their lives in the process.

White women appear to be given better treatment, and attended to with a much more intentional sense of urgency and care especially if they're in pain or during labor, while most women of color are usually made to toughen it out and endure it, under the false notion or belief that they have stronger genes, are much more familiar with pain and painful experiences, and as such, are usually left for longer periods in pain than White women, and this can be seen and proven from the statistic ratio of the pregnant Black and White women mortality rate that the United States releases on an annual basis.

This practice goes further to the fundamental origin of implicit bias in clinics, hospitals, and maternity wards, and is the most subtle yet dangerous form of partial racism that is said to exist in society.

After all, is said and done, the numbers in terms of mortality rate for women of color only keep rising each year despite the technological advancement that the United States health sector makes on an annual basis, and it makes no sense as to why these figures are astronomically large and yet pale in comparison to the minute number of mortalities White-skinned women face when it comes to labor and childbirth.

This is an aspect of the United States that has to change going forward, not just for us in the present generation, but for our children and their children. We must remember that every human is equal and has equal rights, irrespective of skin, race, color, or ethnicity. Despite equal they are not treated equitably. We must teach our children to see color for what it is and to respect it as one of the pure and truly diverse gifts to mankind and humanity. We have to be Color Brave! We must learn to love one another unconditionally, and this is only possible when we begin to question some of the habits practiced in our places of work, from the mechanic's shop to the law court, health cent, or the dentist's office.

America is seemingly a great country, but we ignore that their are not any laid down diverse civil rights for every citizen, and it is only right that we learn to love and respect each other, not just for what we are but for who we are and how unique we are generally. It is for this reason that we should join the fight against racism, and kill ethnocentric beliefs that bring us down. To achieve this, however, unity, love, and persistence are key.

And then she persisted.

14

Having talked about one out of several wrong narratives or notions that our society has for Black women or women of color with a higher rate of susceptibility to pain, I think another important one to talk about would be the narrative that *"Black women do not breastfeed their babies"*.

I began to hear this before I got married, around the time I was a sophomore in college and began to take a proper interest in child welfare, and then I could neither agree nor disagree with this narrative because all of the information I had borrowed or read and not first hand or personal ones. I could not completely relate to it and did anybody close to me who had breastfed before that I could ask, remain curious and optimistic about it till I got married and had children of my own in angst?

One of the lessons I had at an seminar I had attended before I gave birth to my first son had an guest speaker that afternoon, and she talked about every birth being different on every scale and level possible. I however could only completely grasp the magnitude of this statement, after I had given birth to both my sons and could weigh both incidents to scale.

Firstly, Black women breastfeed.

After I had my first son, I breastfed him for the first two weeks, before I could switch him to the baby formula. In his case, he adapted well and thrived happily with it. He was different, and the stress on my breasts was as minimal as possible. The fundamental truth is, breastfeeding can be extremely demanding and tasking, especially if you are a working-class mother that has places to be.

While my first son wasn't a problem to me in terms of breastfeeding, however, the second one was a whole different ball game entirely. I had started breastfeeding him and then ended up overproducing milk for that period, which led me to switch to just exclusive pumping. This was one of the hardest things I had ever done in my life.

For most who cannot get the full picture, I would be attached to my spectra about six times a day on average, and while I would be trying to work, to meet one function or the other in such a fashion, I would be separating milk and preparing to pump another, to avoid leaking milk and having it all over my shirt, which would be a whole new issue on its own.

When you breastfeed, the baby sucks all the important nutrients your body feels he needs and has processed for him into the breast milk he takes in, and this makes your baby grow on a naturally steady balanced diet your body has ordained and deemed essential for production. However, the raw materials used to produce this quality diet your baby needs comes primarily from the foods mother eats.

What the mother if a mother is not well fed, or is stressed out before she breastfeeds her baby, she could feel some really serious pangs of headaches, pains, and extreme dizziness with crazed hunger, because she's feeding her baby with food that would have been just for her nutrition. The baby however sucks at irregular, unprecedented intervals, and could be toughened out or bearable, especially with a mother like me who was overproducing milk as she lactated.

This effect is even worse for mothers who were machine-pumped milk and had to store them in bottles because they were not going to be available due to certain reasons.

In my case, I had to label milk, freeze milk, organize milk and preserve it to the top, satisfactory airport quality and quantity, just so I could move around and attend to my daily chores. I always traveled with my pump.

My life revolved around me and my pump, and I became an exclusive pumper for about 12 months, which was a long and tough period, considering all the stress that went into this.

I breastfed my second son for a total period of 18 months, and I became living proof that Black women do breastfeed.

As an overproducer and an exclusive pumper, it got to a point where my baby couldn't consume all the milk that my breasts could produce before they began to reach the limit and I began to donate milk to about seven other babies, whose mothers needed breast milk as at the time. I was happy to help.

At the end of the exercise, I was able to donate about 10,000 oz of milk to these women, and their gratefulness and gladness cheered me on and warmed my heart, despite the course of the exercise.

I am an avid believer in the fact that overall a FED baby is best. Some may say that a breastfed baby is a healthy baby, but this is only considering what's best for the baby and not the mother. Of a truth, breastfeeding can be challenging, difficult, and as stressful as an 8-6 job can be (or even more to be fair).

As a mother, if you can persist through the pain, and feed your baby with that colostrum in nutrients that he/she needs to be the best, healthiest baby they can be, then kudos to you. You are a real champion. You are an even finer legend if you can donate to this cause. But, this is not required for parenthood. Feed that ba y!

Whatever path you choose, do not follow the ill-notion narrative set aside for you by society. Always remember, BLACK MOMS, DO BREASTFEED.

And then she persisted.

15

I was estranged from my mother for almost ten years before I got to see her face again. It was an unplanned event that came to me unprepared, and it saw me downward spiral for a while before I was able to get my head in the game once again.

My sister who was my informant on all things related to her had suddenly called me saying she was severely ill and had been taken to the hospital. According to her, my mother was found in her home, unconscious and was rushed to the hospital where she spent an extended period getting treated. By the indentures and constant pitch fluctuations I could hear her voice make at the time, it felt like we were looking at something really serious ~ something life-threatening.

As a person who always feels the need and obligation to care for people especially when they need it, I could not resist the urge of wanting to reach out to her and help her in whatever possible way I could. However, I was also scared about my mental health and the possibility that getting in touch with her would not be good for me. I decided then that the cons outweigh the pros in this case.

So rather than physically reach out to her directly to see her or assist in whatever way possible, I decided to still help, but through the most indirect and discreet of ways, I could at the time.

I sent her groceries or money for them through my sister who was with her and made arrangements numerous times to TRY to get caregivers and helpers to clean her residence and hospital, and keep them clean enough to help her push through a speedy recovery. This did not work to any extent. The house was not cleaned, nor was there help when she got home.

My mother did not quickly recover, as she was not just simply sick. If anything, it felt like she would not recover as what made her sick was no joke that could be handled with the wave of a hand.

The doctors found more than traces of alcohol in her system, and there were a lot of other things wrong with her mentally. As well as several other severe problems. Perhaps she had always had issues with her mental health and we just never thought it was something a doctor could see and diagnose. I felt at this point that time was running out to see her and that I would regret it if I did not see her physically. It was then that I decided to call her and see her face for the first time in almost ten years.

When we talked throughout her recovery and her post-recovery plans and I added her back on social media, she was still the same selfish person that I remembered her to be, and it made me regret my decision.

She still made everything about her and made passive comments about us not wanting to talk to her and about not ever hitting us. My mother claims to this day that she never hit us, that she never hit my sister and me while we were growing up with her as children, and it was such a disturbing thing to see and hear.

She was always lying and she said a lot of things that affected my mental health and that made me remember why I decided to estrange her and not talk to her for that long in the first place. I decided to back out of whatever that was for a second, and I saw myself down-spiral my mental health and fall into depression again till I confided in my therapist for help.

Before seeing Lauren, I already began to battle anxiety and depression again and had decided to see my primary doctor, to be prescribed medication to stay afloat, to normalize myself and my emotions, and to be in control.

At this time, barely remembering how my mother's face looked over the phone, the frail and dishonest bit of it made me lose myself and shudder in anxiety, and it took a while to lay hold of my balance and move forward to be the person I am today again.

Lauren challenged me to recognize what I should and should not do, to not give in to pressure and just be myself, and to be confident in myself and my choices. She reminded me of all the good that I had been the past few years before this, 'the good wife, mom, and person, and I slowly but effectively got control of the PTSD and anxiety disorder that meeting my mother again had caused me.

I soon stood back on my feet and sought to chase my dream of helping children who were facing any type of child abuse and psychological trauma. This was what I found joy in and soon, I am consistently working on recovery from all that I had faced at the hands of my mother.

And then she persisted.

16

One of the major keys to this story of my becoming would be forgiveness and reconnection, and I do not think that the story would be complete without talking about all of the people that I reconnected with or forgave despite the ills they'd done to me in the past.

Firstly, I reconnected with my mothers half sister who has been like a mother to me from the year 2020 and all through the pandemic till now. She was one of my strong moral pillars and gave me insight and guidance when I needed it most.

At work, I have three of the biggest moral supports in the persons of Arleen, Ligia, and Margarita, and they are one of the reasons why my place of work has felt as conducive as ever. I still hope to work with them for a few more years as we push each other way beyond the limits society has set for us as women.

I am also very much in contact with people from my paternal side, and I communicate with my aunts and cousins to this day to know more about my Black heritage and Black culture. I am still learning what it means to be Black and to stand against racism as an individual in a society constantly battling its ills, and I keep in touch with them to know the latest news, the history I missed, and to feel the warmth and the richness of Black-skinned people. All my life, I never thought I could affiliate as Black and so the idea still fascinates me today.

If there is one habit I have cultivated over the years, it is to not mix my work life with my personal life and as such, I do not talk about work stuff with my friends and vice versa.

When we talk about racism and gender-based segregation in the workplace, I make sure to cite my points squarely based on what I have seen and faced at my respective workstations and these women (Arleen, Ligia, and Margarita) are the fulcrum of the stable and sociable life I now lead and enjoy at work and I adore them for that.

Another very important person who has made a notable impression on me would be Monica, and our story of meeting and connecting it's just fantastic, to say the least. We met in 2021 through my eldest son.

He suddenly started mentioning the name of a classmate of his, really interested because it was probably the first friend he had that I knew of, and he would always call his name in such an affectionate way at the time.

After a while, he began making requests to go pay a visit to this friend of his, and although I did want him to go, I thought it careless and nonchalant to not know the friend my son was playing with or at least who his guardian(s) were.

This was a virtue I picked up from my career guide/study as a child welfare specialist. When I was his age or even older (precisely through my prepubertal and pubertal phases), my mother did not care or monitor where we went, what we had access to, and who our friends were. This did not sit well with me at the time, but I would always just shrug the feeling off thinking it was just her fully focusing on work and wanting us around her as minimally as possible to not see the 'brat-like' behavior she would always tell us we constantly and continually exhibited.

Then, my sister and I would stay out at a friend's place, in school, or at our boyfriend's house till really late in the night, and her not talking about it probably gave us the leeway to extend this period by a day or two, to see just how much freedom we could get from our ever abusive home this way. We didn't get any reactions from her. None at all. This led my sister and me to know some really bad company and some crazily scary acts, and we were probably lucky enough to both come out of a thing like this unscathed. Some of us still haven't healed our scars from these dangerous encounters.

So when I decided to have a family and raise kids of my own, I had decided from the beginning that I would ensure that I knew exactly who my children's friends were or even go as far as I possibly could into the privy of this knowledge by meeting their parents in a bid to properly monitor and correct any mis-sights I could spot and feel was not good for my kids.

This was how I met Monica, and this was what brought us together till our origins began to overlap in what seemed to us like a friendly suggestion made in the stars and fated to be. It turned out that we'd both had similar stories, which was an option that worked wonders in terms of healing the psychological damage that was caused in the first place.

We spoke to each other a lot whenever we found the chance to, and after we had both shared quite a lot of things about ourselves, she just set into my life and grew on me as a friend and more.

In recent times, she is my 'go-to' person for advice regarding my mother and the nature of our estrangement, and she's always there to remind me of why I'm doing any of the things that I do, to compliment or correct me and to urge me to stay strong irrespective of the situation.

I would also like to add the efforts and influence of my husband Matt on my general well-being and livelihood, as I do not think that I could be where I currently am today without his help.

He always was my backbone and fundamental support in all ramifications and areas throughout my tough times, especially the estrangement periods, and I am forever grateful for what he has done and love him so very much for it.

He was there with me from the very beginning when he agreed to follow me home to see my mother and ask for her hand in marriage and also moved out of Port Huron to keep our families separate and away from all the generational abuse and trauma that plagued my immediate family and maternal home. He was never dismissive of my opinions, nor was he against my estrangement with her, and always corrected/rebuked me in love and gentility.

Additionally, I would like to add a bit about my sister , as she has also been a source of inspiration to me in her own right over the last couple of years.

My sister's name is JoLisa, and she is my younger sister by 18 months. She is also biracial , and understands a majority of the ordeals I have faced over the past three to four decades of my existence as she has been with me the longest throughout these times.

We were both raised under the abusive tutelage of my mother, and we both had to stand strong through this abuse and the derivative psychological trauma that accompanied it.

When Matt and I left Michigan for California after we got married, we sought to bring her in with us as well and bought a ticket for her speedy departure from Port Huron at the time and a safe arrival here. She accepted our offer and arrived in California a few days after that.

Although she does not currently reside with us nor did she do when she arrived in this state, her efforts to be independent and to be a better person that has survived several years of abuse have to be highlighted, commended, and exemplified as it has been unmatched so far. She does strive every day to show the world just how different and better she has been on her own.

We are both of the understanding that our birth mother would always be ours and that nothing could ever change that fact irrespective of careful consideration of the unfair hand she had dealt us in the past. It is for this reason that we have a united front (of sorts) when it comes to caring for our already aged mother, and this was how I was able to provide her with the basic needs and amenities she had wanted during the time she was seriously ill and had needed medical attention due to several complicated issues. I was on a familial estrangement of no contact with her during this time after all.

We had also severally collaborated to provide for our mother on various other occasions before this and without her knowledge, and it wasn't till I decided to virtually call her and reduced our estranged relationship to 'limited contact', that we began to speak a bit on certain social media platforms.

Growing up, my sister did know her father but did not have a great relationship with him, so she was the only family I had during these periods, and, and she means a lot to me.

I am flawed by the fact that she now can independently cater to herself despite the scars from all of the trauma and micro-aggression we were put through as kids, and she now runs multiple jobs in the state of California to cater to her needs and to be the boss of her own life.

I strongly believe that her story of persistence laid side by side with mine can be an inspiration to all those going through trauma or abuse of any sort and seeking to rise out of it victorious. She is an example of persistence and perseverance beyond all odds, and she inspires me to do even more than I currently can and do, as she levels all barriers set for her by her society daily.

And then she persisted.

17

My parents met in Texas through a fateful meeting that was orchestrated by a visit by my grandmother who had at the time gone to see a friend of hers who resided in Texas for certain (presumably romantic) reasons.

She had stayed in Texas for this period (including my father then), away from Port Huron ~ Michigan this time, and grandmother was at the time more concerned with taking in the city air and socializing with the town's folk than returning home.

It was during this particular period that my father met my mother who happened to be just about a year older at the time, and they soon formed this connection that reportedly saw them doing almost everything together.

The period of their dating is unknown to us, but we know they soon developed an instantaneous affinity for one another, and they decided to tie the knot as secretly and as quickly as possible. We are told their Union was a whimsical one.

It wasn't till they returned from the courthouse that my grandmother and her family were told of their wedding, and they had no choice but to accept it as it was. Shortly after this, my father moved back to Port Huron with my mother, and this was where they started a life together and supposedly had me in the process.

Just like I was, my mother was reported 'awfully' young when she got married to my father, and it is said that she had even just finished high school at the time. The rushed marriage or her age was probably why she knew little of my father's innate behavioral characteristics and was yet smitten enough to get married to him that quickly and had rushed into marriage and motherhood without any second guesses. It reportedly didn't take long after they were married, that my father began to psychically abuse her. He hit her so many times, that hitting her to early delivery of me two months before the norm was the last time he ever hit her. I never got to see his face or remember what he sounds like.

When I am allowed to address single folx my age who have a dream they hold steadfast, and want to achieve while they also excel in their marital home, I let them know that it all boils down to vision and desire. It's all in a woman's gift of foresight, and her power of choice. It's all about making the right choices.

When I met my husband Matt, he was not the first man I had dated and he was not my first love.

It wasn't like the man I was in my first relationship didn't care or wasn't loving or sweet. He was good to me during the times we were together for about three and a half years.

He was there through the first teenage wave of psychological trauma and emotional meltdowns that I would usually face, and he would always try to console me the best way he possibly could. But when it was time for me to make the big decision on who I wanted to spend the rest of my life with, I had this feeling, this sense that he wasn't the one. We slowly but surely drifted apart till we eventually realized it wasn't working anymore and decided to officially break it off.

When I met Matt and we spoke to each other for the first time, there was this sense that I could be with him, despite barely knowing him very well at the time. We didn't spend too much time getting to know each other before we were dating, and it didn't take half this time before we decided to get married. It was in the way our ideals and interests perfectly aligned, and in how he told me everything he wanted us to be then and all of his future projections and plans. I knew that was it.

I feel that the first and most fundamental step I took that differed from my mothers was deciding what I wanted to be and what I wanted my future to look like, way before I got married. This enabled me to avoid men with a physically abusive tendency, and always pushed me to be the best I could be in any area or sector I don't myself in. I envisioned through the trauma, the pain, and the abuse, the future me who persisted through it all. And I put in the work every day to see her come to life and continue living with each passing day.

My mother was abused severally by my father, and this was not news to my sister or me from the get-go, because she'll always talk about it and remind us of all she had faced having us be wherever we were and be whatever we became. Even when she abused us, she always made it about her.

The series of prolonged physical and psychological abuse must have started way before my grandmother and had continued to my mother who was determined to bear her children the same fate. I on the other hand was determined to be something different and to make something valuable of my life and my marriage, and I believe that that has been the outstanding difference between the home I grew up in as a child, and the home I am currently mother and wife.

A majority of this story as to how my mother met my father was told to me by my paternal grandmother who I had just recently discovered was family and formed thick bonds of relations. My mother never spoke about meeting my father, what she was doing at the time, or how her life as a child was. She never verbally opened up about anything related to her past, even if there was so much we grew up with the ignorance of, and so much she could have told us. She was and always will be a secretive person (and probably manipulative too). Her reasons for never speaking up to anybody are all shrouded in mystery, and we may never know why she did some of the things she did to us, even though we are all curious to hear her side of the story.

What I do know for certain, however, is that one of my proudest establishments is breaking the generational line of abuse that plagued the female folk on my maternal side, and I was never a part of the 'hand-me-down' micro-aggressive nature that women from this lineage were known to exhibit. I turned out differently.

I am a better mother to my children as I rebuke and correct them in love and absolutely without a shred or iota of abuse. I also enjoy extreme comfort from my marriage to my husband, and he is one of the best, brightest things that ever happened to me for which I am eternally grateful daily.

Despite being married from when we were young, we grew to understand each other to a synchronizing extent that we seldom have spattles or fights over anything whatsoever. We also have two amazing children who mean the world to us and we are both very happy to have them and excited to watch them grow.

In truth, it is not what society dictates is a challenge for a man and woman to be married that defies them of their desired happiness; their ages, the age gap, or their distance from each other. It is rather a mix of patience, persistence, trust, and an ever-increasing yearning to understand one another in love and correction. These are the things that make marriages last through thick and thin and I have been with my husband for 16 years, always remembering and implementing this.

And then she persisted.

18

On one of the few, priceless occasions where I was allowed to speak to women, men, and children of the next generation about the effects of racism, racial aggressions, and abuse, I am always honored to be able to share my story with these people and try to make the worlds better than it currently is and give a bit more to people like me.

In quite a few of my 'Let's Talk About It, With Kenisha" segments, or some of my quite numerous microblogs for the Detroit Moms, I take the time to share what I feel would make a remarkable change to parents and even the kids listening, as they advance through society and communicate with people.

One of the many things I emphasize is educating children especially while they are young, and I feel that this is important because children are not "blind to color" like adults are. They do not know how to hide what they see and are usually open about their observations and thought processes, which makes it remarkably easy and quite socially effective to teach them about racism and acceptance and tolerance at this phase/stage of their life.

Adults, unlike children, choose to be "color blind" and would rather pretend like they do not see color just to not get on the nerves or hurt the feelings of the people they find around them. However, this is the wrong thing to do and an insensitive habit to develop as a child at that age.

It is important to not only "see color" but to accept it for what it is and to learn to love the different shades of color that exist in this world and that we were all created for the creation and enactment of a better world. It is only at that age, the general age of children, that this mindset can properly be created or wrong mindsets overturned with time and patience. It is, after all, quite difficult to teach an old dog new tricks.

Family members have to be taught the key benefits of accepting all individuals for who they are and for what they are, irrespective of where they come from, their skin color, ethnicity, religion, or sexual orientation/affiliation.

I always try to remember whenever I publicly speak and usually take my time to hammer on, is the general support that needs to be shown to all persons indiscriminately, especially individuals of the LGBTQIA+ community.

We have to be their allies and stand up for them when they need it, give them a platform to be heard. We have to celebrate values of love, acceptance, diversity, gender equality and equity, racial authenticity, and variety, and the inclusion of all races, gender classes, and ethnicities.

Finally, I always speak on and for people of mixed heritage. It is one thing to not be racist and to not be "color blind" but rather color brave in identifying all the different types of skin colors there are on the human skin, but there are also those who are multiracial and multi-skinned. A certain study shows that about 40% of Americans do not know how to properly address multiracial/multiethnic folks and usually end up hurting or infringing their feelings and their fundamental human rights.

To the offenders, the key is to always remember that people are people and should be treated equally irrespective of the color shade of their skin. This is important in understanding that people of color or multiracial folx, are NOT to be treated differently or differently just because they look a certain way and sound differently when they talk.

Attaching their success or failure to their skin color, intruding on their privacy to satiate your curiosity by stroking their hair, and all other intentional and/or unintentional practices that are done against multiracial folks should be identified and curbed by possibly nipping them in the bud through sensitization and exemplary practices.

To the offended who are probably multiracial or affiliated with people of color in the monochrome or polychrome, certain things are important to remember as well. There should be no feeling of shame or shame for being multiracial and/or having a different skin color than your peers or classmates.

It is not your fault that you were born biracial, and you have to own your person, your heritage, and your color to be able to achieve whatever dream you have and want to fulfill for yourself. Don't ever let them tell you that you cannot do, or be this person because you look different or are different. We are all different persons bearing different personalities, irrespective of how similar our countenance may be. You are your person.

There is a montra, and "Bill of Rights" have you, I am quite a fan of and am conversant with, and I will share it at the end of this chapter albeit slightly paraphrased, to enable you to understand what you should and should not do.

And then she persisted.

BILL OF RIGHTS
FOR PEOPLE OF MIXED HERITAGE
by Maria P. P. Root

I HAVE THE RIGHT...

Not to justify my existence in this world.

Not to keep the races separate within me.

Not to justify my ethnic legitimacy.

Not to be responsible for people's discomfort with my physical or ethnic ambiguity.

I HAVE THE RIGHT...

To identify myself differently than strangers expect me to identify.

To identify myself differently from how my parents identify me.

To identify myself differently from my brothers and sisters.

To identify myself differently in different situations.

I HAVE THE RIGHT...

To create a vocabulary to communicate about being multiracial or multiethnic.

To change my identity over my lifetime — and more than once.

To have loyalties and identification with more than one group of people.

To freely choose whom I befriend and love.

19

During my period of estrangement from my mother, I remember many people who came to know about it look shocked and surprised that I had done such a thing. Some of them were not happy with me, and the rest didn't even know what the term 'Familial estrangement' meant and was about. It was around this point that I began making notes about familial estrangement, and recommending it to all those who were actually in need of it to get over their scars and psychological traumas.

Now, Familial estrangement is a series of actions due to a choice an individual makes, that involves partly or completely isolating or alienating themselves from some or all of their family members, for a particular period. Decisions on familial estrangement are not to be taken lightly as they could leave a lasting, usually lifelong impression on all parties involved, and are only done to avoid extreme psychological damages or heal fatal psychological wounds.

The reasons for this decision could be for the benefit of this individual's mental health, to escape childhood trauma and heal from it or its fellow, closely related reasons, or any reasons that are on a personal level and that are identified as a stopper to injurious 'person inflicted' activity.

The saying 'family is family no matter what, it is not always accurately helpful and has proven to be fatally disastrous to some individuals who chose to remain in pain because of this reason or excuse. There are several citable examples, where certain persons have been killed by their blood relatives, and it is for this reason that familial estrangement can be recommended when certain therapists or persons see the need for it.

There are certain fears that different people bear about estranging their own family some of which include uncertainty of their children's fundamental years and mental malnourishment away from family if they can and should go with the limited contact or no contact option, if they are making the right decision or if they should go back on their decision to estrange a family member, especially of this estranged person gets sick and could die.

This is actually where therapy comes into the equation.

A qualified therapist must dictate what should and should not be done during an estrangement period whether they were or were not the ones that recommended the estrangement in the first place. Therapists are also really important, as they help the healing process of any individual stranding situations due to whatever reason whatsoever.

One of the things my therapist, Lauren, let me know when I went to see her for the first time about five years ago, was that the most important thing to have enough of during strange times is support. You would need a lot of support as you go through with your decision to estrange that person or group of people from your life.

Depending on the nature of estrangement (whether partial or full), support from family members, life partners, and friends goes a long way to cushion whatever effect estranging this person or group of individuals could have on your social life. Lots of love from familiar faces is highly recommended during these times, as some of the decisions regarding the estrangement that would take place throughout the period would need a humongous bit of care and su
pport, as time flies by over it.

Most estrangements that fail the test of time usually do so because they didn't have the necessary support required to keep up with it and went reportedly back to the individual/individuals they were supposed to be estranged from, during these times.

It is only after having this amount of support and seeking to be estranged from this person(s), that he/she may heal from the trauma indents they are left with, and that they may be able to persist through the suffering and pain, till they can victoriously raise their head in the society, and smile at the things to come in positive anticipation.

And then she persisted.

20

There is no greater healing aid or relief material for any set or type of person who has gone through any kind of traumatic experience whatsoever than therapy. This is something I have and will always endeavor to talk about, whenever I am given the opportunity or privilege to talk to anyone who has suffered any sort of traumatic experience in the past, just like I have. Therapy is always the best, most soothing solution to this hurt and ache.

During the times when my mother feel ill again, and I had to stop being estranged from her for that short period because it appeared to me (to us her immediate family anyway) to be severe and life-threatening, I began to fall into depression and became anxiety-ridden, because I felt her illness would get to the point where I would not be able to see her again, and I started to see myself as the problem. I began to blame myself for her state, and thus began to panic attack and I knew I needed the help.

At this time, I had already begun my therapy sessions with Lauren, and we had gotten close beyond just the professional courteous level. She had already become somebody I could rely on and share my burdens with, and I knew at that time that there would be nobody better to call than her for the situation.

I picked up my phone and called her, relating what had happened to my mother and the events that had ensued after that to her, in a bid to get her to schedule a sort of crisis or emergency therapy with me, especially since she was usually occupied with several appointments at the time of the week when in called her, and I was asking her a favor by booking such impromptu therapy session then. However, I was overjoyed when she agreed to listen to me that day, and I was not to miss that meeting for anything in the world. I wanted a certain form of relief from the emotional pain amongst others that I felt severally at that moment, and I just wished for once that the therapy session would make me relax and get me back on track. I had to hope it worked.

During the session, as she had asked me in a much calmer way and better "set-up" environment now of the circumstances, all the feelings that I had repressed came gushing right back out at me, and I found myself saying things that I had never said before or thought I would say.

I began to accuse myself of my mother's current predicament, and I repeatedly just kept saying "sorry" throughout the therapy session. This must have been because the incident was already then triggering all the memories I had repressed of abuse and all, from my childhood, throughout the stages of my life where I no longer cared what happened to me in my mother's house anymore. It was then that Lauren told me this was simply PTSD.

The amazement came to me there in a flurry and flushed my face with bewilderment because while I knew what PTSD was, I never really thought of it like that or got bothered that it was something that I actually could be a patient or victim of. And I began that day to recount my story to her from the very beginning.

For things and aspects of therapy sessions like trauma reliefs and other related materials, I have a habit of doing things spontaneously when I am anxiety ridden or stressed out. These things could range from having a tattoo done to getting a piercing, and Lauren made me understand that I just subconsciously wanted to remember the pain I had felt in the past, but rather by its owner this time around, rather than let it hurt me or define me.

About spontaneity, one of the most vivid examples I can think of at the moment was getting my nose pierced just as I was about to go see my paternal family for the first time. It was a sort of subconscious declaration to me that I was now in control of my body, including the pain I was then feeling from having the piercing done, and that I no longer needed anybody to give me permission or verification to be who I wanted to be anymore. It was more like an open statement of *"I am not going to be anybody's puppet anymore"*, and my having the piercing done happened so quickly, I had already done it before my brain could completely even record the events of that fateful day.

Another time such a thing happened as well would be when I went to get a new tattoo and eventually a nose piercing, just re-validate the idea that I now had full control over my body, and every one of these times had me riddled with anxiety situations and panic attacks on the verge of breaking.

I had started therapy sessions way before this particular impromptu meeting we had to have on that day, and I wouldn't say that I hadn't told her everything that was wrong with me at that point. I didn't lie or hide anything from my therapist after all. However, that day just seemed so different and happened albeit so differently, that it felt like I truly told her everything I had gone through, and it took a massive weight off my shoulders by doing so.

There were a lot of memories, clustered together and all clobbered up that occasionally acted as a trigger for these types of spontaneous feelings that I felt and that could lead to my poor or rash decision-making phase, especially when I was anxiety-ridden. From incidents like getting kicked down a flight of stairs, to the details of certain inappropriate relationships and communities that I was exposed to as a child which should not have been so with proper parental guidance, and all, the details of this would come crashing down heavily on me, whenever I got triggered by some event that tended to spin such occurrences and the likes.

Amongst these, however, there are a few of them that usually are the most graphic of these memories, whenever I get triggered or vice versa (as I can get triggered just by remembering these incidents), and I remember some of these even as I write these words down because that was how detrimental they were to my mental state and childhood growing up.

One of the most striking would be remembering the details of my grandmother's (mother's mother's) abusive patterns toward us, and the peculiar ~ pain-inflicting way she would hit us that was different from our biological mother, but not by that much.

There were times when she would say we were being bad children, and she would leave us isolated on an entire building floor or story, while we screamed and shouted to be let out and loved and hugged. She would do this just to make her point to us, and no manner of crying and wailing could make her change her mind about this, even if we were to fall from that story building.

I also remember an incident of nonchalance and carelessness, one that makes me question the sanity and responsibility of the adults I had around me as guardians, from when I was of tender age.

In this memory, I was about 4 years old, and I was outdoors crawling and moving around like toddlers my age would expect, I was unsupervised. I discovered a glass of lighter fluid that someone had left outside carelessly, and I was able to come in contact with it and drink it because I was thirsty at the time.

No one even noticed what I had done at the time, and it wasn't till I began to hurt in my stomach from its effects that they had an inkling of what I had done, and took me to the hospital where I got my stomach pumped and eventually treated.

In another memory, I went on a visit mandated by my mother to my cousin's house alongside my sister , JoLisa. The house was a pigsty and was not only dirty but nasty and unkept, with all manner of things piling up the floor to about a few inches off the wall in height.

I was trying to make my way through that section to the back area and didn't see that the parchment of space where I had put my leg had a butcher knife, and I stepped on it. I remember the sharp pain that I felt, and the huge cut I had on my big toe because of the knife. The injury got stitched, and the issue was never raised to my knowledge but was brushed under the carpet.

I was about 8 years old then.

Another graphic one, and probably the most severe of them all, is the memory of my mother once hitting me so hard, I fell from where I was and broke my collar bone. The pain was excruciating.

I was still at grade school here, first grade actually, and I remember having to wear a sling around that arm and going around in school at that time.

There are so many similar incidents like this that I remember, and that I have suppressed and probably have forgotten till the day when I get triggered again, and they come back to my remembrance. A huge majority of my childhood was dealt a heavy blow by sad memories of abuse, racial aggressions, and trauma, and now even as an adult, I still face the effects of those times in what my therapist has confirmed is PTSD, and I try not to remember those incidents or talk about them so much now, so as not to revert to who I was.

Several people are dealing with trauma in our society today, because of something they were made to go through in the past. This event could threaten to change their life drastically for the worse, and might even be weighing them down in society, especially when they seek to tap into their full potential in their career, life, or academics generally. I have seen several persons like this, who have been made Into a ball of sadness by certain traumatic experiences they have been made to go through in their lives.

Whenever I get the opportunity or privilege to talk to these individuals, I always tell them there's no better relief for their troubles than therapy.

Now, therapy sessions don't always work for everybody. I am one of the lucky few to have met a therapist like Lauren who I had an instant connection and who understood me beyond the borders of a normal therapist-client relationship. She is one of the best things that have happened to me.

However, practical therapy isn't as ephemeral or free-flowing as mine was, and mine isn't a general example of what goes on whilst in a therapy session. However, this by no means translates or is meant to encourage an individual to not see a therapist, when they certainly suffer trauma-induced challenges.

Whilst on my journey working with kids who share the same history of abuse that I had as a child, I do my best to expel them from the life of hurt that they no longer

And then she persisted.

21

Racism, gender inequality, Black oppression, and other sociocultural ills and vices that are now present in our society have been formed and were born from desensitization or nonchalance, caused by the general parenting of this generation over the next.

When we talk about racism and/or racial aggressions, gender equality, or even sexism in the truest senses of these words, certain factors make these concepts especially difficult for Black women in society, and that single them out to be oppressed and maltreated. These unfair treatments do not only stop at bland racism even but now go beyond their usual limit to touchdown on issues like implicit bias, especially in places as important as the doctor's office.

A certain study done by the Today health magazine as written by Vidya Rao in the year 2020, suggests that Black women are formed to play against various sorts of stereotypical treatments in most medical settings, and this said treatment usually leaves a toll of negative emotional impression or set of experiences on the women. This effect usually results in Black women in their hesitations when they have to go to a doctor in their time of need, and these women just generally stop frequenting the doctor's, quite outrightly.

Although this dread is now peculiarly and visibly developed by Black women usually against White doctors, it is not limited to them alone, and the ratio of White doctors to Black doctors in the States reportedly weighs about figures of 3:1 on a scale so this concern is said to primarily only thrive within just White doctors generally.

I have personally had various experiences at the clinic where I have been subtly ~ racially discriminated against by the doctor and have felt bad that I thought I was probably never going to show up there again. I usually also (unintentionally) just preferred to work with the female folk, as they were generally more comfortable to work with. It wasn't till much later that I learned, that the female employees who were not only just preferred by me but by about 80% of people who frequent that hospital were getting outrightly marginalized and segregated against by their fellow masculine colleagues and counterparts, who were not taking them seriously because of their gender which was not only distasteful or disrespectful but sickening to the core.

When we talk about Implicit bias, we are referring to the bias systems that are not generally known and are not so easy to spot in American society, and also get overlooked rather than frowned on for a general difficulty to identify and highlight when done as easily as the explicit ones.

While explicit bias would entail the use of the generally/popularly known blatant racial slurs or remarks (such as the use of the N-word), Implicit bias is more about perceptions and those unconscious practices/acts that plague society in a racially segregated manner or sense.

Particularly because Implicit biases are unconscious, they are likely to emerge when individuals have to make abrupt decisions, and there aren't many places that demand thinking on your feet than the doctor's office usually waiting in line with over a dozen other patients while you get attended to as quickly as can be effectively possible.

Studies have shown that most healthcare provisions appear to have an implicit bias in terms of positive attitudes towards White people and negative attitudes towards people of color generally which especially gets worse if this person of color individual is seeming of middle-class in the society.

For Black women, these Biases mean they are perceived as not knowledgeable about their bodies, that they are difficult to deal with, that they do not have insurance or the required funding to cover/provide for their healthcare services, or that they have higher levels of pain tolerance, all of which are assumptions made solely on their skin color and appearance and are just purely distasteful at best. This oversees the clear connection between biases and health outcomes regardless of their economic status, as study after study shows that Black women are not getting the same standard of care as their White counterparts in hospital settings/facilities, especially at places like the gynecologist or the dentist, which are two of the most frequented medical establishment by people of color or multicolor.

For this reason, the average maternal mortality rate of Black women is three times more than it is for White women, and this fact is said to be based on certain assumptions of medical practitioners that Black people are less susceptible to pain and should thus be under-treated for it when compared to a White person.

To make matters worse, when Black women do advocate for themselves as patients, they worry more about being seen as the "angry Black woman" stereotype and thus compromising their healthcare as a result.

The emotional toll of these negative experiences leads these women to a general distrust of doctors and eventually stops these women from going for medical care altogether. This causes several problematic issues for them, especially with regards to "preventive care", and it just continues to outline healthcare disparities time and time again.

The solution however is simple!

If medical students and/or professionals are trained on implicit bias and are taught to be more accepting of the fact that it exists without them having to get defensive or ashamed of this fact, then the subject could be taken a bit more seriously and could be 'gaslighted' to see the situation go under gradually but definitely.

Whenever I am given the opportunity or privilege to address people in the medical field, especially those resident and practicing within America's borders, I always utilize the opportunity to let them know and fully understand that these things do exist and can be stopped, but is only possible with their help. Racism/gender bias exists in various forms and at different levels in our society after all, and it is solely our responsibility to curb these negative influences and eradicate them from our lives for good. I look forward to the next opportunity I am given to speak to medical practitioners. These issues can only be outrightly curbed if we all face them together.

And then she persisted.

Epilogue

I want to start this final chapter, by congratulating everyone who read this book and could make it this far.

I would like to add that while writing this book, I have laughed, loved, cried, and relived my experiences, and this has made it such a fun experience for me. I sincerely hope that it has been that much fun for all who have read this story of my journey as well.

Let me begin this concluding chapter, by talking about why I wrote this and how important it has been to me. This piece is an even bigger relief and therapy to me, and it is a project that has been in the works for some time now.

A few people might have gotten triggered by some chapters, paragraphs, and even a few words in this book. This is simply because, this is not just my truth, but the truth, and this can be a bitter pill to swallow in the face of deceit.

All that this book has detailed so far, has been just the truth, and nothing but purely that.

I began a journey a few years ago to find myself, and find the true meaning and worth of my existence and purpose. As someone who was born biracial, and who didn't get to know her father or her origin as a Black woman, I feel I have a unique purpose in life that I have to uncover. I am a Black woman, who is biracial. My birth and the circumstances revolving around it and swinging me in circles till I got to this point must have been for a reason. I feel that reason was to be a beacon of light and hope to others like me who had gone through abuse and didn't know what to do.

I preach persistence because that is the key to recovery from racial-agression and abuse.

Every day, I push myself to realize my dream of being the best consultant, activist, and professional that I can be, and irrespective of the fact that I might be able to say I'm now living that dream, I still desire to be better and to evolve into something more every single day.

I want to be able to care for those in need, fight against and eliminate racism from this generation, and create a world that is ideal for the next generation.

I want to end stigma, to end racial aggressions, and traumatic stress because I know how terrible these things can be and the heavy psychological toll they leave on all those who fall prey, and it is a terrible way to live life.

Humans ought to live happily and purposefully, in our relatively small bracket of time given to us, and that is what the message of persistence hopes to bring to these individuals. Let this book be glimmering rays of light, that pierce through the darkness of depression and the jagged claws of suicide, and give ambiance to your journey's path lest you stumble on the way.

These passions fueled my zest, stockpiled my achievements, and improved my values, and I want it to be an inspiration and enlightenment to not just those far away, but to those close to me as well.

I desire to be a better friend to my friends, a better wife to my husband, and a better mother to my kids. This is why this road I've taken is not only necessary but essential to complete the path I have chosen to take.

As I got the privilege to speak to several people of all races, cultures, and backgrounds, I began to fully appreciate just how rich the earth is in its diversity, a diversity that its inhabitants are yet to fully cope with, and I began to encourage a through the proper embrace of the various types of people that exist in this world.

This book might be a bit triggering to certain members of my family or be even a lot more triggering than I expect it to be, but I decided a long time ago that these truths must be said, and that the story of my life would be the protest placard against these ills, even if it means saying the hard truths against my own family and saying it in public, just to expose the truths of this matter.

I would not let these reasons stop me from documenting my truths and I will not let them shut me down. From the very beginning, I had thought about what I wanted to write in this book and why I came to write it, and I believe that the pros of citing these examples far outweigh the cons, not just to help me work my way through full recovery and put the life of psychological trauma and a resurgence of all the negative things that has ever happened to me, but to also help somebody somewhere out there, who would be searching for the meaning and light that this book holds and can give them, wherever they may be.

Finally, this book intends to educate, define positive growth, and help stir a meaningful transition from pain to relief, and I hope that all those who read it can take home the positives that the book shares. May love, life and light find you and illuminate whatever darkness seeks to darken your day into night. Just hold on. Remember, persistence is key.

And then she persisted.

~Fin~

Kenisha Coon, MS, (she/her) has lived experience of trauma and resilience in the child welfare system.

She has her Bachelor's degree and Master's degree in Psychology. She has a Post-Masters teaching certificate in Psychology and a DEI in the workplace certification.

She has 16 years of experience in the sector of child welfare and Diversity, Equity, and Inclusion Work. She is a leader of Antiracism and DEI work throughout the country, such as facilitating conversations, training, creating strategic plans, and consulting. She is a graduate of the Minority Professional Leadership Development Program and has collaborated with AdoptUSKids, National Adoption Association, and Families Rising to bring racial awareness and equitable training and education to the child welfare scene.

In her personal life, Kenisha runs a DEI consulting business, Kenisha Coon Consulting as well as a calligraphy business, Lettering by Kenisha. Kenisha volunteers in several communities where the main focus is on expanding and educating of Race Equity and DEI learning to those who may not have had the space to be courageous.

By day you will Kenisha working to dismantle the disparities of Black and Brown youth in the child welfare system and teaching others lessons toward becoming antiracist in everything that they do. By night, she is lettering, doodling, and creating to make folks happy and to nurture her own mental health.

She is a consultant, a speaker, an ally, an activist, a writer, a mom, and a wife.

Her latest project is as the author of And Then She Persisted. The story of overcoming generational trauma, abuse, and neglect. It is the story of standing up against racism. It's a story of advocacy, passion, allyship, and surrendering to stepping into one's purpose.

www.ingramcontent.com/pod-product-compliance
Lightning Source LLC
Chambersburg PA
CBHW020338170426
43200CB00006B/429